Biblical Proportions

Biblical Proportions

Poems by

N.S. Boone

Cover design by Shay Culligan
Cover image by Emiliano Vittoriosi on Unsplash
Facing illustration by Marek Studzinski on Unsplash
Author photo by Lauren Boone

ISBN: 979-8-90146-721-3
Library of Congress Control Number: 2026931913

Kelsay Books
502 South 1040 East, A-119
American Fork, Utah 84003
Kelsaybooks.com

Acknowledgements

Many thanks to the following publications who first printed my poems:

Art Amiss: "A Shudder," "Eye Run," "I did this to myself," "You"
The Auburn Circle: "Direction"
Cave Region Review: "A Clear Blue Arkansas Sky," "Accountant, I," "And Having Done Everything / To Stand / Stand Firm," "The Wisdom"
Far From the Centers of Ambition, Vol. 1: Confluences (Lorimer, 2013): "In-Law" (special thanks to Lee Ann Brown, co-editor).
Georgetown Review: "Out of the same mouth comes blessing and cursing"
The Lake: "Ulysses in the Spirit of Marianne Moore"
St. Austin Review: "God as Columbo," "Oasis : Wife," "They've Outlawed Sex in Europe"
Slant: "Fully Domesticated," "The Ubermensch as Little Jack Horner"
Streetlight Magazine: "Singing Along with Mellencamp's 'I Need a Lover That Won't Drive Me Crazy'"
Teleios: "After One Year of Marriage," "After Ten Years of Marriage," "After Twenty Years of Marriage," "Extending the Metaphor," "Long Time Since Prayer," "Near Death Experience I," "Near Death Experience II," "Near Death Experience III," "When Praying / Folded / A Hunch / A Chill"
Vulcan—A Literary Disallusion: "Filled with / flesh," "The Pork from Within"

Acknowledgements

Preface

It seems that life is constantly about finding proportion, the right measure to use, in each situation, whether in writing, or sawing logs for firewood, disciplining a child, or even talking to a friend over the phone. Thus, the importance of "Proportions." As for "Biblical," you'll notice quotations from the biblical text smattered throughout the poems. That's because, as I try to remain open to the calls of consciousness from all quarters as I write, the biblical text takes precedence as that one I've been drawn to most. Other texts come in to play as well.

These poems are expressions of consciousness in the moment of composition, a clearing of the clutter of normalcy into the openness of thought as it touches the world. I'm trying to say something I couldn't possibly say in conversation, or in an essay or story. It's sometimes emotion recollected, no doubt, but not recollected in tranquility—not at all—but in the tempestuous, swirling, chaotic, and inescapable vacuum of now. And it's more the shape or the form of the feeling recognized in the constant flux of time that will, I hope, be understood from these words, and will thereby be of use.

William Carlos Williams was right when he said, "There is no poetry of distinction without formal invention." The poem is the only space in culture wherein we can experiment with thought-language (the two are not separate). An essay may express a new or different idea, but is not free to allow language its breadth of play. A story is bound too much by the demands of plot or character. But the poem is an open field, limited only by the meagerness of one's imagination or linguistic resources.

The poet crafts the syntax, the lines, the rhythm, pressing against and sometimes through established boundaries of expression, seeking the form that allows for the maximal expression of the thought as it is felt, or the feeling as it is thought. The poem is the experience of the experiment on the blankness of the page, the freedom of that moment—the freedom to bind oneself to the form of one's own making. No other avenue of language is so open to the invitation of invention.

The more we characterize the poem as rhyming tetrameter quatrains, or, more commonly today, as arid left-aligned monosyllabic expressionism, the more we are impoverished of ingenuity, and the less we have to pass on to those who will be overcome by our future.

Contents

Accountant, I

All those years to have missed
the measure in Christ

inescapable as exact
        as impossible as
        adding a column of zeros

    for not by calculation
                neither credits
                nor debits
                neither ones
                nor zeros

                love

the measure you use, he said, it shall be measured against you

                perfect

        as He is
        as inescapable as
        I am that
        music of motion’s moment

                poetry

                justice

Weighs and Means

It is the need to be elegant
which perturbs

weighs and means

I have shed much blood, he said, but
you, my son, will be a man of peace.
Erect, my son, the house of God.

What's inside's
mere material
sodium, potassium
or, everyone's favorite,
serotonin.
Motion's the mystery
can't be weighed.

Fit into her dress, finally
the wedding day
had to lose eighteen pounds

All the closed systems
potassium, sodium
the harpist's fingers' motions
my serotonin
aah,
how nice, how safe
and my mutual funds outperformed the market again.

But to extend
beyond fingertips

It is the fact of your life
that you changed
an inspiration
living
beyond serotonin

Weigh my words
beyond angel's flashing sword
and grunts and groans
beyond birth

Means peace

Poverty

Stricken / eye
plucked
crooked back
his hands outstretched
he said *The Requiem*
if he could only hear it once more
would unfold
his life

Touched
every / time
he said he turned his back on God
he cried ; the rejection
the form of the act
of it
Sprung up / stone's echo in a deep well
or the first time in the ocean
the wave surrounded and
took me under head first

I know the Lord
I know the Lord
I know the Lord
has laid his hands on me

Stung / the man's stunning size
cigarette in hand about
to die
once said
"God damn death that we have to die"

And "I can die now I just begun to live"

Born / to live
they sing in field in unison
and clap with cotton-pickin hands

Did ever you see
the like before?
It's Jesus preaching
to the poor!

Funny Money

It's fun to think about money, who has it, who doesn't.

It's fun to think what you might do with it if you stumbled into millions someday, plowing the field of hope and letting money plant its seeds.

It's fun to think of your company matching your 401K contributions, and of how you can stop working because of it.

It's fun to think about all the debt that slides through fingers and machines all day long, just numbers zipping through cybernetic screens, tallying up, up, up.

It's fun to think of the national debt. It's so much fun I have to laugh each time.

It's fun to think how we scrimmage for it, like a rugby match, striving for those points, against all foes, thrusting ourselves headlong into what consequences? Head traumas? Broken necks? Shin splints? Divorces? Alienated children? Or the touchdowns of success, second homes, and Alaskan cruises.

It's fun to think how it is meaningless—just pieces of paper on which words are scribbled, various codes, cultural monuments, symbols. Sort of like a poem. Sort of like this. Something to be exchanged, backed up by fiat of soldiers' arms.

It’s fun to think of all you could exchange for this—the sound of a mountain stream, an eight-point buck lifting up his head before running off, the spiral of a woodcock over a field of waist-high grass at sunset, the twinge in your gut at the sight of her that day, and all you imagined about God or the devil, and what you think you know of yourself.

It’s fun to think of this as money. Go ahead, put this in your pocket. Walk around with it today. Let it give you the comfort and security of a fat wallet. Trade on it, or try to. You may find it can be traded for many loves, backed up by the full faith and credit (and arms—I have a shotgun!) of The Poet.

It’s fun to think of money as poems. Go ahead, put some bills away in a book on your shelf. Pull them out at night for long contemplation before bed. Decipher their codes. Think how the numbers add up to something consequential. There are no accidents, only symbols. All can be exchanged; all will be exchanged in the scrabble to make up for the primal debt we can never pay off.

Shakedown

by the rivers we wept

That there is a plan
shake down
to the body / mind
to live up to

World without end / Amen / Amen
Build a railroad / Build
a bank / Vision is prophet's
profit / never bankrupt long
as I can see / the light

may my hand forget its skill

flip the switch
on the circular
saw, squeeze the
forearm in a vice,
cut it off, all
of it.

To his face, I saw it.
Called him a hypocrite.

whether in the body, I
cannot tell; or whether out
of the body, I cannot tell:
God knoweth;

Boys will be / boys

And Having Done Everything / To Stand / Stand Firm

                    With the word
                            how
                            make it
                            hold

Pines do whisper and
he meant it when he said
he was hotter than a pistol

                            Against schemes

          100-fold return
          Word into thing

They have killed all the prophets and I am the only one left
                                                                                          to stand

Stand in the sun
                    on the highest rock
                    closer to the gods on brochures—
                    Oh, Sedona—how
                    does it feel to sell
                                        souls?

A foothold gained

Nobody knows the trouble I've seen
Glory! Hallelujah!

Against schemes

And when I told her the news
she laughed
And when he asked her she said
No, I did not
But he said Yes, you did laugh

Laugh

Descartes' Supermarket

In my mind God
        is bald,
            65ish, . . .
muscular chest, maybe with
                                        a silver throne, . . .

I can't tell
            for certain—anyway, . . .

                                            maybe just steel. And angels have large,
                                                            awkward white wings,
                                                            and everyone stands on
amorphous ground . . .

of clouds. I think
I want pizza,
            Sunkist,
            those avocados look good . . .

I think the cashier's
                              just had a break-up, . . .

                                                            or she was late . . .

At any rate
she needs my smile
as she hands back my credit card.

I think I know what I want,
what she wants.

I have an idea of heaven . . .
My feet feel my idea of the ground.

When Distance Is Lost

No grass
just partially
cotton underfoot
polymers
—or—in or—

Steroid chicken En Masse
barely see the sun

TV is real with academic presentations /
Mosques and churches with art of all qualities

Deception's implacable
(but I know now how
many trees are in the yard—
whether bark is smooth—how
many steps from the back porch to
the fence on the property / line)

Pointillism
traffic—jam—integrity
one spot among other spots

not emotion, really
an integer
among other integers
—fin—in fin—

It’s not *Guernica,* nor
exactly time for tea when
the man said
“I have something to expiate; / a pettiness”

    Integrity / taking
                    place

A Shudder

Cold shudder before sleep
                bodies what occasion
                of memory of guilt of cold
        in the garage
                no heat
        and slipped screwdriver split
        knuckle suck it up
                says Dad or
                just a memory
                squinting eyes

Or swollen ankle's
                cause for imposition
                make her get a pillow
                                    prop it up
                                    only to shudder
                still

From inside or outside or
                simply one
                organic moment
when I burst into
                form

                                    You can't pour new wine into
                                                                old
                                                wineskins, he said

O   Lord pour
me into another
        shudder

I did this to myself

If another time the same circumstance arose
I would not choose this.
But forgiveness of self
is a statue crafted for commission,
poised forever in the wrong moment,
a selfishness wholly forged from unrighteousness.

Cathartic/Selfish

Holding up the needles tipped
with my bleeding eyes

The body must live on, the mind
breathe its own stupidities
in full knowledge and displeasure
and await the dip in time's forgetfulness,
the only way out of hurting me, myself.

All the sudden the chain slipped off the saw, right in the middle of the cut. Then off came the casing and the bar so that all I held was the handle and a running engine. I had forgotten to tighten the nuts. I'm so stupid. And this was just weeks after I had almost killed myself trying to start a fire with gasoline and had then told myself how stupid I was and how I had to be more careful.

The Pork from Within

Blood
to the frontal lobe
cut off, adrenal glands firing
argument afterwards feels
guilty as sex.
I guess that
evil in me feels
good to yell
like bread that
evil in me feels
good that evil
in me

Virtue has gone out of me

To have it back
in word
when word and moment
diverge.

To be spoken for by spokesmen,
an idiot, in the Greek sense,
and dumb in any sense.

To walk alone at eve,
a repetition, getting up
alarmed for the day. No
moment found appropriate.

And yet it held
too long, the word
spoken inappropriate,
inauthentic—held
in consequence, in guilt,
perhaps in suffering
to be redeemed. That woman
who touched him, would she
give back, now immortal,
all those years of blood?

Indignant, I yelled, "I hate
you!" and ran to my room
as he watched the football
game.

Eye Run

Snap
dragon pop
corn split
the word
image split
screen double
feature dance
into shaky language rum
ba black sheep
what we are hum
bug splattering out
of which we came
                    consoling
                    eye runs
up trees
obfuscating twin
ing thickness of dark
branches, leaves,
unable there to dwell.

Thus to chop pic
nic table or bird
house into a clearing
stand within to see fo
rest from trees. Im

age but what's splintered
is not of use, can't
be bolted, planed, built
into but split and
you've got at least fire
wood for warmth and
to watch its light
                                burn.

Watch Your Language

How it builds
          builds always
                    an edifice around
                              you

like the thick glass
                    of skyscrapers
seen through from the inside
but reflects your face, the sun,
everything from the outside

How it shields you
                         (Watch it!)
blunting edges of thistles,
                    engines,
                    canines
manufacturing models of planets,
                              cars,
                              cares

Watch that it doesn't fall,
this tower built from all
your life, all you
                    've been and have
                                   n't always known

Lifts you up tall
aboveboard
gilt trim and stylish
even

Watch it vault to conclusions
faulty
even

No matter,
it can be a faux fireplace
incorporated into the decor,
flair

Watch it smash all attacks,
boulders and birds
flying into it,
falling to the foundations

Watch it ascend, steadily
growing through years
of practice

Watch it keep you straight

Watch it, then, slide out
from underneath itself,
snakes underneath the rocks,
the stones begin to rustle
like dead leaves sound like tails rattling

(then a rumbling)

hissing passion—
mortar crumbles
hissing desire—
a stone dislodged
hissing God
beams are bending
hissing nature
crackling glass

(then bombsounds of implosion)

(only God could do this)

Can't even see through the smoke and debris

hissing
(only nature could do this)

"Out of the same mouth comes blessing and cursing"

And "the tongue,"   he was saying
    "sets on fire the whole course of nature
    and is itself set on fire by hell"

which is not any more impossible

    than substance and accident
    when communion is telephoned out
    and sell-a-vision shot in   even the church!

    that thoughts entertain devilish cruelty
    and heroic deeds of charity

    that the lifeblood flowed out the razor cut
                                                    in merely a moment!
                              (a grave live with flowers and insects)

But that wonder of silence, of sleep,
of dreams wherein I'm bald or my head is shaved
against my will, the antagonism
of myself and time

But that accident produced me
one night in a conjugal embrace
during the blizzard of '77 in Dugger, IN
              OR
Providence slipped in:
purpose or accident:
"A cosmos," he said. That's me,
baby, burped
    by God

“unspeakable words, which it is not lawful for a man to utter”

I had sex before this
writing beside myself through
toes pulsing out
of me mind muted.

She strolled the beach depressed and with no language
to share her vision, her art a failure.

I once ate the contents of an entire 16 oz container
of chocolate icing: 2,600 calories,
115 grams of fat, 380 grams of sugar.
So what? At most I’d gain a pound.

Sensation’s constant tide, feverish
chill and warm, chamomile and muscadine is
sex without love—a failure of art.

A successful nurse at the children’s hospital,
she seems relatively attractive by all common standards, but
she vomits her meals. I can’t say a word that will stop her.

Submersion is poetic.
Tells everyone goodbye.

Sugar butter salt is good. Over 2 million years
of evolution tells me so.

And I went unto the angel, and said unto him, Give me the little book. And he said unto me, Take it, and eat it up; and it shall make thy belly bitter, but it shall be in thy mouth sweet as honey. And I took the little book out of the angel's hand, and ate it up; and it was in my mouth sweet as honey: and as soon as I had eaten it, my belly was bitter.

Filled with / flesh

in purgatory
blind
scales
to balance
to will
spiritual eyes
will turning tide
to submerge
my great city
fishes
It often threw to eat
the boy into open eyes
the water submerge
to kill him. in tears of saints
The father said, joyous
Help Thou
my unbelief! My great city
And when land
it came out what's left
of the boy on her withered
he was as bosom *he said*
a corpse, flock *I buffet*
but he arose black birds *my body*
when taken to gorge *daily*
by the hand. great supper of God

in purgatory
blind
scales
to balance
to will
spiritual eyes

Arise, Peter! Kill and eat!

Either way, identity's unsure.
There's a murderer within
just as there's a murderer without.

Contract!
Curl into a ball and sleep
on the roof.
Close your eyes.
Know the action
of your blood.
Feel stillness in your heart.
Know the motions
of the policemen on your street
and of your wife and your animals.
Let them be.

Then, stretching
out arms and yawning,
face in the sunlight,
the sky nearer, full
of color like the peaches, full
and round and bending
the limbs to the ground, bending
down in the night . . .

Cast to the other side.
The net bursting with
the weight of fish.
Bloodied hands pull
in as much as . . .

Arise!
Cast across the Earth.
Grid the sphere.
Take the peach off
the limb.
Pluck the grapes off
the vine.
Gut the fish.
Swallow the snake's
tail forever.

No Dome

The music of spheres
we would need to give up
our bodies to hear,
earless, only knowing

(Let all domes henceforth
lie supine)

You'll hear enough
of the music   in touch

In touch, don't listen
don't say anything
let the chickens roost
where they may, even
in thy tousled hair

let the poem die
with you, lie with you

a chemical component of being
let it free to do its work that
you will never know

I'm a child what a child wants
I'm a child

(what child wants

chilled

(dome no dome

****

It's the dream of every child
the domicile of mother
a base desire
"the sea is not our home"
to drown the world
so Noah can make us
in his image
to call forth all animals together in one
ship—and God's eye is the sun.

But the babble he wanted
and the broken tower
calls us to our bodies

(lions, giraffes,
penguins)

nipples to feed, feet
to kick, teeth to
fall out of punched mouths
minds to build a missile to
pierce the dome
a missile to send us
back to the body
the cockroach
what's wrong
with rain on my ears
with crawling?

(good
people
care
enough
to
argue)

Long Time Since Prayer

What am I not seeing?
What am I not?

What lack in value?
What lack in love?

What blindness to the "features of men's faces"?
What shadow between the motion and the essence?

What excrescence, gap in my teeth?
What fear?

What marred harmony to keep my singing low?
What force masters me?

What a thought! That one can be a Christian for decades
upon decades.

Or is it only in a moment, a twinkling of an eye
a tension in the decision

a torque in the hip, a limp
or leap with the knife toward all you've known and loved?

Is it only in prayer and silent listening
or always away, permanently receding in front of cataracted eyes?

"One wonders, but not well"
living without God in the world, like hell.

How could I?
How could I be so lost?

When Praying / Folded / A Hunch / A Chill

Speaking like
this needs covering
me with me for
warmth doesn't want
uncertainly to be
left here without
me to hold onto
a burning crisp
crumbling
in hand unfolded

Extending the Metaphor

If God had said to me
You are a dog
I would bark and bark
until my voice would rasp
until my throat would bleed
and the concern of my friends
and associates would turn to indifference
And I would, on all fours, sniff
and scavenge with impoverished nose
and would make-believe
I was meant to dream
of yesterday's grease-encrusted T-Bone

Until that woman talked back to him,
eyes straight on his face—*Yes,*
but even dogs eat the crumbs
from the master's table—
extending the metaphor
as any woman, any man speaks
words in force derived from his
original

God as Columbo

And the LORD said unto Cain, "Where is Abel, thy brother?"

Because he knows, from the beginning,
from the slightest residue of your guilt
left at the crime—

because he knows, he does not judge
but calls you from a distance,
providing every chance for confession;

comes 'round day by day
probing your conscience,
your feelings, inescapable,

like one of your grandfather's bear hugs
that would suffocate
even as you'd feel the tenderness in the squeeze.

By the time you know he knows
and you have no choice but surrender,
you realize that you've always wanted to confess

as your ego shrinks to the size
of the notepad he keeps in his trenchcoat,
and you want just to be kept there through the night.

Leaves of Ash

the leaves
fluttering past the faces of my friends
turning in the hands of my friends
by the fire as we read by its light.

All but ashes is fiction:
November snake covered in leaves,
my thoughts on eternity:
cerebral play spiraling electronic
out of associations—word by word—
even the Word of the Lord.

My thoughts on the beauty of fall:
that as great as he is, God
cannot destroy it all.

A Clear Blue Arkansas Sky

That the sky is blue
is not beauty,
not an illusion
either but the human
fact of perception
from the eyes gripped in
the skull, chained to the brain,
limited receptors of all there
is. And all there
is for me as I walk out of the
office, having been flooded
all day with fluorescent
light, and look to heaven
so that I'm not in Arkansas
anymore nor at the office nor even
in the parking lot: I am standing on
the rocks of the earth, my body
breathing praise of the sky.

Falls City

Forget Falls City
and forget the natural light of stars
and moon-glow on the undersides
of breeze-blown poplar leaves.

Forget Falls City
and forget the dirt-caked feet,
the dirt in the beer,
the same dirt's micro-organisms
lining the stomach, settling in the bowels—
all we're made of—forget that.
Forget the earth.

Think of the future, which, as everyone knows, is plastics.
What you will, what you won't,
what ought to be in mind, in mind.

Forget Falls City
and forget literal straw men
stuffed for mischief on country roads at night.

Think of the future
and why the shape of youth must be an arrow
sharp enough to pierce all pleasures, bleed out
their fine integrities
(what is, what ought to be, what ought)

and why the arrow slows, dulled,
suspended in air, free to fall to the ground
we never learn to land on, stand on, be on
(for what lies beyond)
Falls City

Plans

To plan an emptiness in time
is childhood
gone
never
here

segmented each moment
into expectation

Connect the dots: abstract plan's
emergent forms revised, applied,
and essence deciphered, GTAC,
research and experiment, TAGC,
that's better, biological forms
evolving by digital patterns,
digital networks extending human
consciousness, nothing's immediate.

More like Connect Four on the floor
a planned child, economists predict
an expenditure increase as means
increase, rearrange the marbles is
what's left, CATG, that's okay.

Predictably I started wearing shoes
for every outdoor venture the very
day my bare foot smashed into a thistle
plus the genetically inherited
sensitive feet soles from my father.

He said, You
fool! This very
night your life
will be demanded
from you.

And while I'm feeling dead, I'll tell you of
my dog just coming into maturity
that died and that, with some shame, admittedly,
I cried on more than one occasion—
even more in fact than over a friend's
child, statistically another SIDS victim—
the sadness so hard to deaden when
unexpectedly life is taken.
E. A. Poe died relatively young
and he tried so hard to explain it all
but we remember of him his perverseness
which falls upon us in a doorway's shaft
of light—an evil eye when we don't know
what to do so we smother it and go
back to bed.

I demand an apology.

It's dead, but did it ever live?

Near Death Experience (I)

You are dead
Blunt trauma
Gun shot
Heart stopped
Suddenly, with no pain
You've floated above your body
See it on the bed
The sidewalk
Bathroom floor
You think of your sister you haven't seen in years
Suddenly, you're above her in the supermarket near
Where she lives in San Diego. She's being handed a cake
Decorated in silver and gold
Or you keep floating above your hospital bed
Above the building itself
Where you notice a lone sneaker on the roof.

You are dead
You are not free, yet you feel no compulsion
Just warmth that lifts as it envelopes.

The lights above are beautiful, bright
Shining with no shielding of eyes
You move toward light
In light, in joy
Suddenly pain

In the darkness of the body
On the bed
The bathroom floor
The sidewalk
It’s a tunnel.

Called back
What do you know
What to do now
To survive.

Near Death Experience (II)

You are dead
The only thing that wakes you is an alarm
Shrill and mechanical
Repeating, repeating
Daily, deadened, arising to routine
You speak, searching for kindness in your voice
You listen, searching for wisdom in waves
You touch, searching for love in bone and tissue
Working, you rise as if the stairs were mechanical
Eating, sleeping
Shrill
Repeating.

You call your sister to tell her
About the cake of silver and gold
She's amazed
You tell the nurse about the shoe on the roof
They find it
They have questions for your answers

What is its goal if the grave is not?
What is its goal if the grave?
What is its goal if?

Questions asked with no answers
Answers given that tame and diminish with age
Shrill and mechanical
“I hear an army,” you think
Coming in waves
Repeating, repeating
Never retreating
Through the tunnel
Alarmed for the day
Another day
Just another day
What to do
To survive.

The Ubermensch as Little Jack Horner

My name is Nick. Maybe
that's why for as long as I can
remember I've worn Nike shoes.
My mom would take me to the shoe
store where I would sit on
a bench and a man wearing
referee stripes would take
my foot's measurement with one
of those weird steel contraptions.
The Nike's always just fit better. And then
there was their slogan, "Just do it."
It took me years to realize its gravity.
It worked so well. More chocolate cake,
Mom. "Just do it." I want to see the Grand
Canyon. "Just do it." New sound system
for my car. New car. I was a superhero
just figuring out my powers as I entered
into the banquet hall of adulthood,
the butlers in referee stripes circling
the sequined dresses and tuxedos holding
trays with martinis or small sandwiches.

Wife and children? Or maybe a dog
first? Labrador, like your first pet? Or go
trendy, an Australian Shepherd. “Just do it.”
How long will you keep
the apartment? There’s the house
on the cul-de-sac with fruit trees
in the backyard. Swimming pool? No. Too much
to worry with just now. “Just do it.” The dream
job, vacations, cruises all over
the world’s oceans. I hadn’t noticed
water was covering the floor,
the sequined dresses were sloshing,
my feet wet and cold inside
the Nikes. The chandeliers were farther away
than ever and brighter. I looked
for a corner, asked a butler
for a pillow. “Just do it.” Maybe
a blanket. And the darkest corner.

You

Control's not static
sticks even
to change
loose to ooze over
everything
even
you letting go

Near Death Experience (III)

In my dream she was alive.
I saw her walking along a street
with shops and restaurants, chatting
intensely with friends I never recognized.

She was dressed not in white,
but in her favorite style for shopping,
a splashy, colorful blouse with fluttered sleeves.
Not young and angelic, she was 60ish,

her hair subtly permed. She wasn't
surprised to see me as she drifted
over and we sat at a bistro
table in the shade, though it wasn't

hot. Some force from without seemed
to restrain my emotion, my voice.
I could only tell her how sorry
I was that she had to miss

her newest granddaughter's first birthday.
She never took her eyes from me.
She was serene, happy—the age
of having grandchildren to brag

about, the age of her confidence,
of her leisure. And she said, "Every
little thing I'm there." I couldn't
say all I wanted to say, couldn't

spill my emotions, nor repeat all
the carefully crafted phrases that she couldn’t
hear or understand on the hospital bed.
I had questions to ask, but only

sat there witnessing her glory, subtle perm,
splashy blouse, friends to chat with,
things to do. When I woke
I knew it was the last

I would see of her. And
I thanked God as I cried.

Platonic Meditation

This wind is amazing she said
and I talked of what we should
do and what we had not done.

She seemed to rise
as she walked, her skirt
lifting up slightly

as I had not noticed.
The time was filled
in my talk—energy

to say to her who cared
about poems. Then
roseate splendor, her

skin I didn't notice
when I could only
think about poems.

Bowling

When Pete Weber or any other
PBAer screams in stylized ecstasy
after a strike, I think of love
and the difficulty of repeatable actions.

And the time she turned
and kissed me on the stairs
and held me in the hallway
of the high school and how
that moment holds me still.

Bowling offers not many
variables—certainly not like
team sports' unpredictable
opponents or strategies, or
even golf, with wind and turf
conditions such that a
perfectly repeatable swing
may not yield success.

Or that she's a vandal
with her blunt will
I love her she swats
away convention I hate her
she pushes through my desires
until she turns toward me
mysterious I love her.

In bowling the conditions are
not completely precise, but
there's limited variability, so
it seems that a score of 300
ought to be more common for
professionals, though you
rarely see one on TV.

We use ten pins because Congress passed
anti-gambling legislation forbidding nine.
Genius. Add a tenth. Keep on bowling.
Throw a strike, dance in wildly printed pants,
and when she rolls down the lane bump against
her smooth, polished skin, then tumble and fall
for anything, like she's a bowling ball.

Singing Along with Mellencamp's "I Need a Lover That Won't Drive Me Crazy"

Speeding between the endless fields of corn and beans
70 . . . 75 . . . "This old junker might make it to 80" . . .
I need a lover that won't drive me crazy
I sang it, shouting it, shoulders and head rocking.

I was cradled between those cornfields so well
I could love the song and the singing
and feel secure, even when speeding,
so that the world would blur into color and sound
as I jetted on my desires.

Yet behind the words were the truths all singers know:
seeds don't always stay where they're planted,
the tallest cornstalks can't reach the sky,
and there never was a lover who wasn't crazy.

Love Memento—

cheap plastic magnet
STUCK
ON
YOU

    Open,
        the empty fridge
    lights up limited possibility
    of eggs for dinner;
    defrost the bread in the
    freezer for toast

Kiss
  you on the alter
Grounded
  underneath the headboard
  your lips and mine—

Only
    You said
    Everyone is meager
    as a lemon zester.
    Of what use our
    fingernails our lips
    but to scratch and to kiss
         and
    I love being in your
               limits

In-Law

It's not emotion
I feel
          the cloud descending
               white

eyes bending with the mountain,
the sun behind—
ALL LIT.

What action's down in the valley—
cars coursing through the warpings of time,
the fallen ridges,
Unaka Ave.
There's golf in Buffalo Valley.

But,
      today foot-slide
side soil of Roan Mt.

Foot-slip
         up
     Mother-in-law's mouth
     born in the shadow of the Roan.

     Speaking slip-up
     splash outward
              from rock water
             (What goes up
                    must come)

Don’t dare dance
    just stand if you can

Breathe mountain
        on Unaka Ave.
    takes you
            to Unicoi
                if you can
                    get there
                        go.

After One Year of Marriage

I, at the age of 23, am expanding.
Last year, in fact, I doubled in size!
"You may kiss the bride . . ."
A bride I became, and doubled.

There is a point at which I will stop.
I will begin to be old then.
I will wrinkle and shrink—all wrinkly and shrunken.
But I may or may not be larger than I was at 18 when I'm 81.

Over the vast interiors—(or are they exteriors?)
Over the soul and the spaces between souls (which are occupied by ???)
These are expanses wherein we dwell
And we expand over our prime (and wrinkle and shrink thereafter).

And the two shall become one [flesh]
But is it flesh only?

Oh, I've been expanding (so long as my soul is I)
And the doubling (did it have to be instantaneous?—the kiss?)
And the agitation, the butting in (Hey! these are my spaces to occupy—get your own vacant and vast expanse!)
But we are one! We are obligated!

Oh yes,
Expanding is hard work.
Walls must be obliterated.
"More room in here! We need more room!"

For I promise never to expand into another as I do into you (this is commitment),
For our resources are unlimited.
Space, you see, is endless (and, thank God, timeless—the soul, the soul is timeless!)

But the fear . . .
Expanding is hard.
Hard little shell,
Vital enough to push out the edges
Making all very solid, hard.
A monolith.
Interior—strong, solid.
Expanding is hard (in the sense that it's difficult, and I don't want to be bothered with it just now).
No encroachment, please!
And it is simply fear . . .

But on a Saturday morning one year after
"You may kiss the bride . . ."
(Can you believe it? I've more than doubled in size!)
Our cozy flesh is at least a bit entangled
As we lie a little longer than is reasonable.

Fully Domesticated

Gradually the tarantulas danced away
after one reared and showed its fangs
and was shuttered in a box.

And the foxes trotted off
that fought with our wild cats
for after-dinner scraps.

And the raccoons sheltered in place
when one was shot
before it could escape.

And the wicked chorale of the wild cats
heard on weeknights,
gone.

And the heated words by the microwave,
sarcasm over the cutting board,
that dish broken on the tile floor.

Gone, too, the pillows of sweat,
the curses that were prayers.
God, what word is there

that does not sound Greek?
Something less than *passeth understanding*;
something more than pharmacology.

Recovering Christian

There's wine with my cereal.
I read Apocalypse in eggs and bacon.
In any house, many items need repaired—

the door to the linen closet sticks and remains open,
and there's a broken baluster at the foot of the stairs.
Will the television bring news of brotherly love, or lack thereof?

I fear the Holy Ghost in you, the tongue of flame
that told the truth about me once;
and once, in your anger, showed the truth about you.

The bath is filled with children's toys.
Will the axehead float tonight?
Who will fix the closet door, the baluster?

We are careful and troubled about many things,
but only one thing is needful.
Don't call the carpenter.

After Ten Years of Marriage

It's no great accomplishment, to live with another for a decade.
Don't pat us on the backs, anyone.
People and animals of all sorts live with annoying, destructive diseases for years on end, and some parasites spend whole life cycles under the skin of other creatures.
That eagle Dillard writes of may still have those weasel jaws hanging from its neck after a decade.
Commitment? A weasel clinging to each of our necks? The old ball and chain?

But to expand into another, to live with another,
not as a dead chain, not as mechanically as a weasel struggles to keep its death-jaws clamped, but as nothing else, as no one else can or has before.
And we've done it.

To be grooved as we are into new patterns of consciousness no one could, or would, ever dream of!
That we tighten ourselves like drums ready to be verbally beaten when we hear our name loudly spoken.
That we stop each other cold and abrupt with the way we hold our eyelids, brows, slightly tensed.
That we snort a laugh at the mere mention of "husky."
That new people roam the earth stamped unalterably with our love.
We have made new creatures, we have made even ourselves new!
(Behold!)

No thief can break in and steal you as he did your diamond ring.
You're in me, always.
Nor can I buy you back as I did your ring if you are ever taken
from the earth. The loss is irrevocable, as will be my sadness.

Because for the years we're granted we shall grow like roots
and branches
out from each other to the sun, or into each other, vining around
each other,
grooving ourselves into the brain and blood—a oneness no science
can predict.

(When I cleared out the fencerow, I cut down most of the trees and left a few. And as I was grinding down the stumps and the roots that were visible at the ground's surface, I realized that I couldn't decipher whether a root was connected to the tree left standing or the tree cut down. I examined the roots to find they were so interconnected that it was impossible to determine which tree they belonged to. They were of both. Yet one tree was gone while another remained. The roots remained with the remaining tree but the tree that is gone shall never return.)

Husband Frustrated at the Time Wife Spends on Smartphone

I am a man, skeptical of all
except myself. She is a woman,
given to authority, not tense and
skeptical about it, not instinctively

recoiling from the impositions of
knowledge and control. And so we
came together, and for years
grew together, she intrigued

by my aloofness, drawn to
my sense of self-sufficiency,
lone and rebellious in the face of the
world. And she loved me because

she could trust me, my instincts
for self-preservation, so strong,
would keep her safe as well.
Was it simply years that wore

away my strength? Was it
that little by little I forfeited
my soul to daily toils and money
concerns? For a while the children

drew us closer to each other,
to protect them against the world.
But as they grew their own
resilience, we began to realize we

weren't needed. Did we need each
other? And as we groped about in
the dark puddles of our nights,
there appeared, as if dropped

between us from heaven, a black
monolith of knowledge and authority.
My instincts kicked in immediately
to recoil from even its shadow,

sensing already its consequence.
It would shatter me, but it would
have her, all of her. The allegiance
came slowly. At first, she was

skeptical, too, of this new
source of power. In curiosity, she
scrunched her face up closer and
began to listen. Scoffing a little

at first, she'd laugh with me
at its claims, superciliously.
I would laugh and scoff with
her, sensing already that in time

I would be the one scoffed at,
broken into incoherent dogmas,
shouts and pleas she would not
be able to hear, for attention

had shifted. I could not join
her in her credulity and keep
my integrity, my self-assurance.
It was all I had that had

ever attracted her to me, save
the children. Now, there was nothing
to share. Just me, myself, aloof,
alone—not enough to satisfy. I

wonder how it ever could have
been enough. But it was! It was
the magic of love, passion, of two
souls sharing life intimately. The

intimacy, now broken, like an
adultery. Jealous and powerless
in inarticulate protest I stand by
watching my life break apart

before her, feeling my blood go
cold each night as she bathes on
the rooftop in the warm glow
of blue light, opening herself

to all the messages of all the
twinkling satellites, the new stars.

“I came home to my husband a different woman”

—having read M.C. Richards—

But I remember he had been telling me about golf.
He was told after
wormburner, wormburner, wormburner
scooching across the turf, couldn’t get it up,
that it was all in his grip.
One must feel the grip,
the club not a forged thing, but an extension of the hand.
I listened.
Silly, and nothing so mystical as that.
Just the marriage of two very unlike things.

Disjunctive notes, atonal chords,
words, just sounds, pouring out.
Not too long and I could grasp each one.

Kept coming back to the piece
(35, again at 43. At 36 and 37. At 43 like I was 35 again.)
never finishing.

In a dream I could catch them so quickly I was giddy.
One and another and another.
My hands against the scales and gills not breathing on the warmth
of the sun-glint surface.
One and another,
’til a voice said
They’re not alive.

“A big fat lie, that Mother’s only sleeping.”
I said I think it’s 1 Thessalonians 4.
“Really? Read it.”
. . .

"A big fat lie.
Read it again."

"More slowly," she said.
The . . . . . . Ra-ven . . . still . . . . . . is . . . sitting

In a dream I
plunge to grasp them cold and deep living and writhing
mucous membrane my fingers
they slip away
plunge again

A month of celibacy, then another

Spending hours preparing meals now
slicing vegetables slowly with feeling

Spending time too much time
the fingers in the right places
the words, one then another, no more
fat on the bone

Wet fingers
sticks
the words in place

After Twenty Years of Marriage

> *Two men will be in the field; one will be taken and the other left. Two women will be grinding with a hand mill; one will be taken and the other left.*
>
> —Matthew 24:40–41

I do not know the day or the hour
When I fell into love with you.
But I did fall.

What must be clearly known by now is the fact of aging—
That after twenty years we are not the same and never will be again.
And to look back
And to remember
How hard we were, so that nothing could penetrate—
Neither of us would let anything in, unless we desired it.
We were hard against the world, and we had our ambitions, and we went after them.
And we were, at first, hard against each other,
Two diamonds paired together, with points that sparkled
and would cut.

How hard! Against the world, and not able to integrate each other.
The fights were hard.
And we tangled enough to find that we cannot now be unwound from each other.

When did we begin to soften and integrate, losing the hard edges?
We wade into the water of the world rather than plunge in to swim the course,
But we splash each other, and laugh, and enjoy the cool of the evening in each other's love.

There have been billions who have married, lived together, loved each other, and died lost.
I had always believed that I would not be among the lost.
I do not know the day or the hour
That I lost myself in you.

The Fig Tree Withers

If the fig is a purple-in-moonshine gift
then regard me also as gift
dull flame
to spread
as death to spread as joy
and only mind to separate
and only body to bleed
and only the mockingbird
this moment's chuck-and-rustle

to die again in delight.

The fig-gift : Fool! That which thou soweth is not quickened
except it die.

Sow with me through this night fig leaves
to recognize ourselves as mystery
to press imagination through its illimitable chambers
and against the barriers of the holy.

If you can bless me, consecrate my tongue-in-cheek
gift me cookies-and-cream, on-the-field elation
and memory of all those loves.

They buried him, and why not, in his Wal-Mart uniform.
He loved his job and the people he saw every day at the store.
"But if it dies it produces many seeds."

The fig-gift : mystery : to let it consecrate
the absolute death of absolute life.

Oasis : Wife

Where shall I turn?
To the one my heart loves.
Deep inside where the fire burns,
I return to the one I love.

How high must the eagle soar,
Or how far roams the lion,
Before coming back to nest or den?
How many nets cast by the fisher?
        All empty!

But I return to you, love of my life,
To abundance. Oasis. Wellspring. Wife.

They've Outlawed Sex in Europe

They've outlawed sex in Europe.
It's easy to see why—
It's violent, patriarchal,
And inappropriate for the eye.

They've outlawed food in Europe.
It's barbaric that we still
Butcher plants and animals
Instead of taking pills.

They've outlawed jobs in Europe.
No employer has the right
To hold its workers hostage
With a paycheck day and night.

Universal Basic Income
Is now the people's creed.
With free pills, a roof, and internet
What else do they need?

They've outlawed thought in Europe.
Just know that you are equal.
All the studies say the same thing:
Discrimination is thinking's sequel.

They've outlawed death in Europe.
How nice it now can be.
If the body quits its functions
You'll be hooked up to a screen

So that you'll be only consciousness—
No more bloated, bloody corpse
To hang around the neck of Mind
(Footnote: Hegel is our source).

They've outlawed life in Europe.
It's all just too obtuse.
Just imagine how much one life *takes*,
Whether codger or papoose.

Life is just too selfish.
Humans are energy hogs.
The blue earth goes round without us
On the galaxy's gears and cogs.

Ulysses in the Spirit of Marianne Moore

Not the itch of idleness nor the golden
idolatry
of swashbuckling calculus sets us out to sail;
but nature fails to appoint our ways,

though hummingbirds can guide us across
vast sea gulfs
by their tiny beating wings or even trees that
never stop reaching out and up may

crudely point towards that subtle
chastity
which drives us out of bed each morning or sits us
upright at dinner with our elbows off

the table, or out of our seats in the
presence of
a stranger just entered the room. These longings
will never be illicit, the substance

of distant stars that frames us, empty
yet upright.
So it is that ventures of seeking and finding
never yield but vessels that need refilling.

Direction

The door faces north.
Into the cold wind
I take the dog

out for a leak,
but he pees before
I can attach the leash.

I would have led him
to the east around
the corner where he

could have dug at the roots
of the locust tree,
or barked at the neighbor,

or nobly stood wide
and strong, nose against
the wind, sniffing

all the possibilities
of January. But I
call him in, hang

the leash on the hook
for another dog,
another direction.

The Wisdom

in fantasias unconscious
in songs already sung
to know proverbs and enigmas
the words of the wise and their riddles

that if wisdom be vanity
then come down from there

out of safety
to walk in the counsels of style

            the one way

opened forth in the going
the turn of the eye

instantaneous to the urgency of perfection
to risk not truth

not to wait
but grip down and begin

to know wisdom and instruction
to perceive the words of understanding

moment's maturity, multiplication
branching, bringing forth what

now can be. "You are skilled
in what you do," he said,

"and that is, live."

Notes

"Accountant, I": "the measure you use . . ." comes from Matthew 7:2.

"Weighs and Means": "I have shed much blood . . ." refers to 1 Chronicles 22:8–10.

"Poverty": "I Know the Lord Has Laid His Hands on Me" is an African-American spiritual, also quoted in the last four lines. "God damn death that we have to die" and "I can die now I just begun to live" come from Charles Olson's poems, "The Thing Was Moving" and "Moonset, Gloucester, December 1, 1957, 1:58 AM," respectively.

"Shakedown": "by the rivers we wept" and "may my hand forget its skill" come from Psalm 137. "Long as I Can See the Light" is a song written by John Fogerty, of Credence Clearwater Revival.

"And Having Done Everything / To Stand / Stand Firm": The title comes from Ephesians 6:13–14; "They have killed all the prophets" comes from 1 Kings 19:10; "Nobody Knows the Trouble I've Seen" is an African-American spiritual; the last lines refer to Genesis 18:15.

"When Distance Is Lost": "I have something to expiate . . ." is from D. H. Lawrence's poem, "Snake."

"A Shudder": "You can't pour new wine . . ." is from Matthew 9:17.

"Virtue has gone out of me": The title is from Luke 8:46, also referred to in the poem's last lines.

"Out of the same mouth come blessing and cursing": The title and first lines come from James 3:6–10; "A cosmos" is from Walt Whitman's "Song of Myself," #24.

"unspeakable words, which it is not lawful for a man to utter": The title is from 2 Corinthians 12:4; the final lines are from Revelation 10:9–10.

"Filled with / Flesh": "Purgatory Blind" is a poem by Charles Olson. "It often threw the boy . . ." is from Matthew 9:22–27. The "great supper of God" is from Revelation 19:17. "I buffet my body daily" comes from 1 Corinthians 9:27.

"Arise, Peter! Kill and Eat!": The title is from Acts 10:13.

"No Dome": "the sea is not our home" is from William Carlos Williams' poem *Paterson,* Book IV.

"Long Time Since Prayer": "features of men's faces" is from Gerard Manley Hopkins' poem, "As Kingfishers Catch Fire"; "what shadow between the motion and the essence" echoes T. S. Eliot's "The Hollow Men"; "a twinkling of an eye" refers to 1 Corinthians 15:52; "a torque in the hip" refers to Genesis 32:25; "One wonders, but not well" slightly alters a line from the poem "kitchenette building," by Gwendolyn Brooks; "without God in the world" is from Ephesians 2:12.

"Extending the Metaphor": "Yes, but even the dogs . . ." is from Matthew 15:27.

"God as Columbo": "And the Lord said, . . ." is from Genesis 4:9.

"Falls City": "Think of the future . . . plastics," refers to a line from the film, *The Graduate* (dir. Mike Nichols, 1967).

"Plans": "You fool! This very night . . ." is from Luke 12:20.

"Near Death Experience I and II: The descriptions come from various near-death experience accounts. "What is its goal . . ." references "A Psalm of Life," by Henry Wadsworth Longfellow. "I Hear an Army" is the title of a poem by James Joyce.

"In-Law": "Unaka" is a corrupted form of "Unicoi," a Cherokee word for "white." Unaka is a prominent street in Johnson City, TN. The town of Unicoi lies just to the south. Roan Mountain, where my mother-in-law was born, is in the Unicoi range.

"After One Year of Marriage": "And the two shall become one flesh" is from Matthew 19:5.

“Fully Domesticated”: “passeth understanding” is from Philippians 4:7.

“Recovering Christian”: “We are careful and troubled . . .” refers to Luke 10:41–42.

“After Ten Years of Marriage”: reference is made to Annie Dillard’s essay “Living Like Weasels.”

“I came home to my husband a different woman”: A woman, I don’t remember her name, said this happened to her after reading M.C. Richards’ book *Centering: in Pottery, Poetry, and the Person*; “Mother’s Only Sleeping” is a gospel song written by the Stanley Brothers; “The Raven still . . .” is from Edgar Allan Poe’s “The Raven.”

“The Fig Tree Withers”: The title refers to Matthew 21:19; “Fool! That which thou soweth” is from 1 Corinthians 15:36; “But if it dies . . .” is from John 12:24.

“The Wisdom”: “To know proverbs and enigmas . . .” is from Proverbs 1:6; “grip down and begin” comes from William Carlos Williams’ poem “Spring and All”; the final quoted lines come from Adam Piper, who taught a Bible class on Proverbs that I attended.

About the Author

N.S. Boone teaches literature and writing at Harding University in Searcy, Arkansas, and is the author of *Understanding Jorie Graham* (U of South Carolina P, 2025). He preaches most Sundays for the Magness Church of Christ in Magness, Arkansas. *Biblical Proportions* is his first book of poems.

www.ingramcontent.com/pod-product-compliance
Lightning Source LLC
LaVergne TN
LVHW090534110826
845146LV00003B/1093

* 9 7 9 8 9 0 1 4 6 7 2 1 3 *